ANCIENT GREECE
REVEALED

Written by
PETER CHRISP

DK Publishing

LONDON, NEW YORK, MUNICH,
MELBOURNE, and DELHI

SENIOR EDITOR CAREY SCOTT
SENIOR ART EDITOR JOANNE CONNOR
PROJECT EDITOR EDDA HENDRY
ART EDITOR REBECCA JOHNS
EDITOR SARAH GOULDING
DESIGNER JOANNE LITTLE
PHOTOSHOP ILLUSTRATORS LEE GIBBONS
JÜRGEN ZIEWE
MANAGING EDITOR CAMILLA HALLINAN
MANAGING ART EDITOR SOPHIA MTT
CATEGORY PUBLISHER SUE GRABHAM
ART DIRECTOR MARK RICHARDS
PICTURE RESEARCHER LORNA AINGER
JACKET DESIGNER CHRIS DREW
JACKET DESIGN EDITOR BETH APPLE
DTP DESIGNER JILL BUNYAN
PRODUCTION CONTROLLER DULCIE ROWE

First American Edition, 2003

Published in the United States by
DK Publishing, Inc.
375 Hudson Street
New York, New York 10014

03 04 05 06 07 08 10 9 8 7 6 5 4 3 2 1

A Cataloging-in-Publication record for this book
is available from the Library of Congress.

ISBN 0-7894-9271-7

Color reproduction by Colourscan, Singapore
Printed in China by Leo Paper Products

See our complete product line at
www.dk.com

CONTENTS

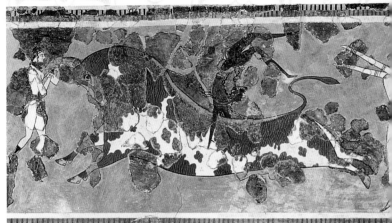

The Greeks lived on a mountainous mainland and hundreds of small islands scattered across the Aegean Sea, as well as on the west coast of Anatolia in modern-day Turkey. After 800 BC, in search of land, trade, and adventure, the Greeks spread out even farther, founding settlements on the coasts of the Black Sea and across the Mediterranean.

Pendant in the form of a pomegranate, a fruit

DIG DEEPER
Archaeologists found this beautiful little gold pendant on the island of Cyprus. It is from the Mycenaean period, an early Greek civilization that dates back to 1600–1200 BC. Archaeology itself comes from the Greek words *archaios* (old) and *logos* (knowledge).

THE GREEKS

MORE THAN TWO and a half thousand years ago, the people of Greece developed one of the most advanced civilizations of the ancient world. The Greeks introduced the alphabet to Europe, and invented politics, science, philosophy, theater, athletics, and the study of history. Their stories and plays are still told and performed today. We know more about the Greeks than almost any other ancient people thanks to their writings, which were carefully preserved and recopied by hand by Christian monks. More information comes from the excavation of towns, palaces, temples, tombs, and shipwrecks. Greece was conquered by the Romans in the second century BC, yet the Greek legacy lives on to this day.

Temple of Athena at Paestum

Rider carved in marble

PLACE OF WORSHIP
Greek temples, with their rows of stone columns, are instantly recognizable. This one was built in about 500 BC, in a Greek settlement in southern Italy. Thanks to archaeology, we know that it was dedicated to the goddess Athena. Many small pottery statuettes of Athena were dug up around the temple, where they had been brought as offerings.

PARTHENON FRIEZE
This carving comes from the most famous Greek temple of all, the Parthenon. It is part of a frieze that, set up high, went around the central part of the temple. The riders above are on their way to a festival held in honor of Athena.

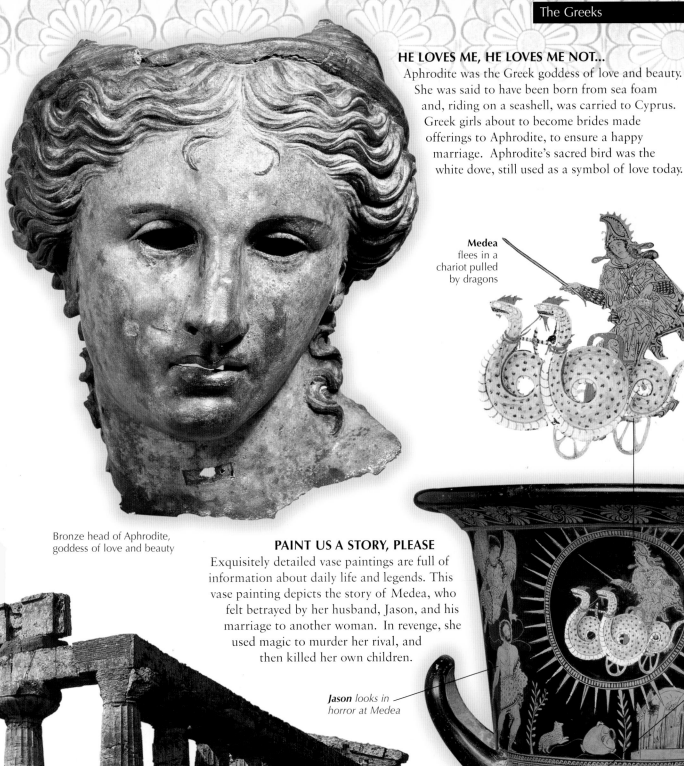

HE LOVES ME, HE LOVES ME NOT...

Aphrodite was the Greek goddess of love and beauty. She was said to have been born from sea foam and, riding on a seashell, was carried to Cyprus. Greek girls about to become brides made offerings to Aphrodite, to ensure a happy marriage. Aphrodite's sacred bird was the white dove, still used as a symbol of love today.

Medea flees in a chariot pulled by dragons

Bronze head of Aphrodite, goddess of love and beauty

PAINT US A STORY, PLEASE

Exquisitely detailed vase paintings are full of information about daily life and legends. This vase painting depicts the story of Medea, who felt betrayed by her husband, Jason, and his marriage to another woman. In revenge, she used magic to murder her rival, and then killed her own children.

Jason looks in horror at Medea

The nurse mourns the dead children

TROJAN HORSE

THE ANCIENT GREEKS left us many epic tales. One of the best-known is the story of Troy, a city captured by the Greeks with a clever trick. They built a wooden horse, which they left outside the city. The Trojans believed the horse was a peace offering from a surrendering army, dragged it inside their city, and began to celebrate. However, hidden inside the horse was a group of Greek warriors. That night, while the Trojans slept drunkenly, the warriors crept out. They killed the guards and threw open the city gates to let in the Greek army. Soon the great city was in flames, and the 10-year war was over.

EXPLORING THE TROJAN HORSE

1. **Pine:** *the wooden horse was built from plentiful pine*

2. **Epeius:** *skilled craftsman and chief builder of the horse*

3. **Wheels:** *for moving the huge horse when it was finished*

4. **Guards:** *to ensure no Trojans saw what was inside the horse*

5. **Garland of flowers:** *to show that the horse was an offering*

6. **Odysseus:** *cleverest of the Greeks—the horse was his idea*

7. **City gates:** *finally opened to let in the Greek army*

8. **Walls of Troy:** *the city was surrounded by high ramparts that had kept out the Greeks for 10 years*

9. **Wine vessels:** *from the Trojans' celebrations*

10. **Trojan soldiers:** *drunk, asleep, and easily overpowered*

THE MONSTER OF MINOS

According to legend, the Minotaur was a monster—half man, half bull—that lived in the Labyrinth, a maze beneath the palace of King Minos. Theseus, a young prince from Athens, went to Crete to kill the monster. When Arthur Evans dug up the palace at Knossos, he found images of bulls everywhere. Perhaps the legend has its roots in an ancient religion that worshipped bulls.

The hero Theseus
kills the Minotaur

Owl   Dog

Monkey

ANCIENT BEGINNINGS

GERMAN ARCHAEOLOGIST HEINRICH Schliemann believed that the legends about the Trojan War were true. In the late 19th century, he searched for Troy in Turkey and excavated at Mycenae in Greece, hoping to prove his theory. Instead, he discovered a previously unknown civilization. Called the Mycenaean civilization, it dated from the Bronze Age, and lasted from around 1600 BC until 1200 BC. English archaeologist Arthur Evans excavated in Crete between 1899 and 1931, and discovered an even earlier civilization, dating back to before 2000 BC. He named it the Minoan civilization, after Minos, the legendary king of Crete. Both civilizations produced rich royal palaces and beautiful wall paintings, jewelry, and pottery.

PALACE OF MINOS

Arthur Evans uncovered the vast palace at Knossos in Crete, the largest and most important of the Minoan palaces. The palace walls were decorated with frescoes, paintings giving us glimpses of Minoan life and religious worship. Evans rebuilt some of the upper levels, such as this colonnade, based on the style seen in Minoan paintings.

MINOAN CRAFTSMANSHIP

During the Bronze Age, Greeks did not know how to use iron, but they were highly skilled at working in soft metals such as bronze and gold. This beautifully crafted Minoan gold earring is very large—almost 6 in (15 cm). It shows two dogs standing on the heads of monkeys, ringed by other animals.

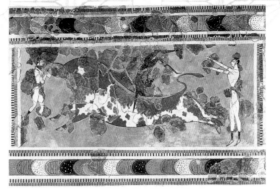

EARLY ACROBATICS

This wall painting from the palace at Knossos shows athletes gripping a bull by the horns and hurling themselves over its back. Perhaps this dangerous sport was part of Minoan bull worship. Two of the figures are women—in Greek art, females were shown with white skin and males were tanned.

Double-headed snake

Dolphins from a wall painting at the palace at Knossos

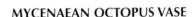

MYCENAEAN OCTOPUS VASE

Although the Mycenaean civilization developed in mainland Greece, Mycenaeans settled and traded all over the eastern Mediterranean. This vase decorated with an octopus comes from a settlement in Rhodes, one of the most easterly Greek islands. The swirling yet orderly pattern of the tentacles is typical of Mycenaean art.

Copy of a painting of a bull hunt

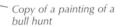

Mycenaean vase made 1400–1300 BC

Death mask of a Mycenaean king from around 1600 BC

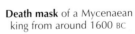

MASK OF AGAMEMNON

According to Greek legend, Mycenae was ruled by Agamemnon, the leader of the Greeks at Troy. In 1876, Heinrich Schliemann found a royal grave at Mycenae that contained the body of a man wearing this death mask. The mask was made of fine gold, pressed over a wood carving of the face. Schliemann was convinced that he was looking at Agamemnon's face. However, it is now known that the mask dates from at least 400 years before a possible date for the Trojan War and Agamemnon.

HOME OF THE GODS

The top of Mount Olympus, Greece's tallest mountain, was said to be the home of Zeus and 11 other famous gods. They were called the Olympian gods. From their palaces high above the clouds, they looked down on the lives of men and women. The gods took an interest in human affairs, often helping their favorite heroes.

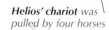

Helios' chariot was pulled by four horses

LEGENDS AND MYTHS

ANCIENT GREEKS WERE fabulous storytellers. Their myths—a word that originally meant any story—have entertained listeners for thousands of years. The Greeks told stories of gods, monsters, and heroes to make sense of their past and the world they lived in. Every important Greek city had its own mythical heroes, such as Bellerophon in Corinth, and Theseus in Athens. Their deeds were told as lessons to inspire noble behavior. Myths were also used to explain events in nature, such as thunderstorms or the daily movement of the sun across the sky. Above all, the Greeks loved a good myth, retold in a poem or play, for its wonderful entertainment.

Bronze statue of Zeus, king of the gods

FLY, PEGASUS, FLY

Pegasus was a winged horse that Bellerophon, a prince of Corinth, tried to ride to heaven. However, Zeus, king of the gods, sent a horsefly to sting Pegasus. The horse bolted and Bellerophon fell back down to earth.

Pegasus on a Corinthian coin

MIGHTY KING OF ALL THE GODS

Zeus's throne was on Mount Olympus. The Greeks believed that Zeus caused thunder and lightning, and described him as the "cloud gatherer" and "hurler of thunderbolts." He had many love affairs, with goddesses and with mortal women, and fathered dozens of gods and heroes. Zeus often appeared to women in disguise, as a bull, a swan, or even a shower of gold.

CHARIOT OF THE SUN

The Greeks explained the sun's daily movement across the sky with their story of Helios, the sun god, who rode his chariot across the sky from east to west every day. In one version of the myth, Helios returned to the east every night by floating back in a large golden cup. The people of the island of Rhodes made Helios their most important god.

Odysseus listens to the beautiful song of the Sirens

THE STRONGMAN

Heracles was the son of Zeus and a mortal woman, Alcmene. Even as a tiny baby he displayed great strength, strangling snakes in his crib. As an adult, he was set twelve labors, or seemingly impossible tasks, by the wicked king Eurystheus. One of the labors was to capture an enormous boar alive. Heracles brought the boar to Eurystheus, who was so terrified that he jumped into a large pot.

Heracles carrying the boar

Eurystheus cowering in the pot

ODYSSEUS AND THE SIRENS

After the Trojan war, the hero Odysseus encountered many adventures as he tried to sail home to Ithaca. Among the perils he faced were the Sirens, terrible creatures whose irresistible singing lured sailors to their deaths. Odysseus made his men plug their ears with wax, but had himself tied to the mast of the ship, so he could hear the Sirens' beautiful song without jumping overboard and into their clutches.

Jason is swallowed by a dragon

THE GOLDEN FLEECE

Greek myths often have a variety of versions, with different plots. Jason, for example, was the hero who was sent by Pelias, king of Iolcus, to find the Golden Fleece. The fleece came from a magical flying ram and was guarded by a terrifying dragon. In the version shown on this vase, Jason was swallowed by the dragon but saved by the goddess Athena. He then returned to Iolcus and gave the fleece to Pelias.

Spaces between words are indicated by three dots

GREEK WRITING

This Greek inscription describes divination, or telling the future, by watching the flight of birds. On their travels, the Greeks came across the Phoenicians, a trading people from the Middle East. The Phoenicians had their own alphabet, which the Greeks copied and then improved. They invented new letters, including signs for vowels, which the Phoenicians did not have. The Greek alphabet is the ancestor of all European alphabets.

GREEK REVIVAL

AFTER THE COLLAPSE of the early civilizations around 1200 BC, Greece entered the Dark Age—a time we know very little about. The Greeks stopped writing, making fine pottery, or trading with other lands. However, around 800 BC Greek civilization began to revive. Traders took to the seas again, carrying cargoes of pottery and wine. Villages grew into the first cities, such as Athens and Sparta, and settlements were founded around the Mediterranean. Greeks developed a new alphabet and began to mint the first coins in Europe. This revival, which lasted from 800 to 500 BC, is called the Archaic Age.

Phoenician text recording the building of a shrine

PAINTED POTTERY

During the Archaic Age, the Greeks developed new styles of pottery, with beautiful vase paintings. A Greek vase was both a practical object and a work of art, often signed by its painter. Such vases were popular all around the Mediterranean and have been found in places as far apart as Spain and Egypt.

A potter painting a vase

Steering oar

Vase painting of two wrestlers, around 500 BC

Glass pot

MONEY MAKES THE WORLD GO AROUND

Coinage was another foreign invention adopted by the Greeks. The first coins were made in Lydia, in what is now Turkey, in the seventh century BC. The use of coins made trading a lot easier. Previously, most traders had to barter, which meant that they could only buy goods if they had something that the sellers wanted in exchange.

Greek coins stamped with the symbol of the city that produced them

PERFUME POTS

Greek merchants traded in pottery, wine, oil, and luxury items such as this pot for perfume. The perfume was made from olive oil that was infused with rose petals or spices.

The tortoise, symbol of Aegina

CHANGING TORTOISE

In around 600 BC, the Greek island of Aegina made the first Greek coins. These were decorated with sea turtles, which were then the symbol of Aegina. After Aegina was conquered by Athens in 457 BC, the islanders stopped being great seafarers. They switched the symbol on their coins from a sea turtle to a tortoise, which lives on dry land.

Eye painted on the bow for good luck

SHIP AHOY!

This vase painting shows a Greek merchant ship, able to carry a large cargo under a single square sail. Big-bellied ships like this were slow and vulnerable to pirate attacks. They sailed around the Mediterranean and Black Seas, carrying grain from Sicily and Egypt, copper from Cyprus, ivory from Africa, incense from Arabia, and slaves from the shores of the Black Sea.

PARTHENON

THE PARTHENON, which stands on a rocky hill looking down on the city of Athens, is one of the world's most famous buildings. It was built almost 2,500 years ago as a temple to Athena, goddess of the arts and guardian of Athens. The entire building was carved from sparkling white marble, and it was decorated with magnificent sculptures painted in bright colors. Inside stood an immense statue of Athena, with ivory skin and clothes, and armor of solid gold. Every four years a great festival was held, and a beautiful robe, made by expert weavers, was brought to the temple as a gift to Athens' favorite goddess.

1

2

EXPLORING THE TEMPLE

1 **Marble:** *24,250 tons (22,000 metric tons) quarried north of Athens*

2 **Columns:** *46 columns in all, each 36 ft (10.5 m) tall*

3 **Pediment carving:** *birth of fully armed Athena, daughter of Zeus*

4 **Metopes:** *carved painted panels showing Lapiths fighting centaurs*

5 **Armor:** *Athena is shown armed— the whole temple celebrates Athenian achievements in war*

6 **Nike:** *human-sized statue of the goddess of victory, giving Athena a wreath for victory over the Persians*

7 **Statue of Athena:** *40 ft (12 m) tall, with a gold robe and armor, and ivory skin*

8 **Snake:** *may represent Erichthonius, a legendary king of Athens*

9 **Plinth carvings:** *birth of Pandora, the first woman in Greek myth*

10 **Procession:** *weavers bringing a new peplos (robe) to Athena during her festival, the Panathenaea*

Ruins of Apollo's temple in Delphi

THE TEMPLE OF APOLLO

The Greeks thought that their gods could give them practical advice in the form of oracles—forecasts and advice from priests and priestesses, who acted as mouthpieces for their gods. The god Apollo delivered the most famous oracles, at his temple in Delphi. People went there from all over the Greek world to seek help.

RELIGIOUS WORSHIP

DELPHIC ORACLE

At Delphi, worshipers asked Apollo their questions through his priestess, who sat on a three-legged bronze bowl. She then went into a trance and gave the god's answers. Greeks asked oracles a variety of questions. One of them worried, "Will I end up in the gutter?"

THE ANCIENT GREEKS took religion very seriously. They believed that life was influenced by powerful gods and that it was important to win their support. There were various religious ceremonies, all aimed at pleasing the gods and gaining their help. Most of these ceremonies took place in the open air, in front of temples, which were seen as the homes of the gods. Worshipers often stood beside a raised stone block—the altar—and presented gifts to their god. These gifts included liquid offerings, called libations, as well as food. The most important gifts, however, were animals such as oxen or sheep, which were often killed as sacrifices to the gods.

A TOAST TO THE GODS

The priest on the left holds a vial (offering bowl), which he uses to pour liquid onto an altar. These libations (ritual pouring of liquids) might consist of wine, oil, milk, honey, or water. Libations to gods were also offered at the table in Greek homes before every meal.

A fire was lit on the altar

HONORING THE DEAD

It was believed that providing the dead with a proper funeral helped to ensure that they did not come back to haunt the living. Funeral processions to the grave were led by women. They tore at their hair, wept loudly, and sang *threnodies*, songs of mourning to lament the death. In many parts of Greece today, women still sing special weeping songs at funerals.

AN OX FOR THE GODDESS OF HUNTING

This religious relief shows worshipers bringing an ox to an altar. Here they would sacrifice it to Artemis, goddess of hunting, hoping to win her support. Some of the meat was burned on the altar so that the rising smoke could carry the gift up through the air to the goddess. The rest was cooked and eaten by the worshipers at a feast in her honor.

Artemis with her bow and quiver

Vial, or offering bowl

Child worshiping

Dead warrior receiving a helmet from his wife

BIG AND SMALL OFFERINGS

Worshipers who could not afford to sacrifice an ox to a god might offer smaller gifts, such as these little figurines. These were left at a temple of Artemis by Greeks who wanted to please her. Today, Orthodox Christians in Greece leave decorative objects called *tamatas* in their churches.

Stag

Figurine of Artemis

MAY THEY REST IN PEACE

Greek ideas about what happened to people when they died changed over time. What did not change was the belief that offerings had to be given to the spirits of the dead, to help them rest in peace and ensure that they did not come back to haunt the living. This jar, containing oil used to anoint the body, is such an offering.

Lekythos, or oil jar, found in the grave of a warrior

Funeral procession

DOUBLE PIPES FOR THE PLAY

Music played a big role in Greek theater. The most popular instrument was the *auloi*, or double pipes, which accompanied dances and songs during the play. We know from descriptions that there were different styles of ancient Greek music. However, the Greeks did not write their music down, so we can only imagine what their music might have sounded like.

The auloi had sound-holes along each pipe

GREEK THEATER

THEATER WAS INVENTED by the Greeks some 2,500 years ago. Many words relating to theater are Greek in origin, such as theater itself, mime, pantomime, tragedy, comedy, and drama. Plays were put on as part of religious festivals, usually in honor of Dionysus, god of drama, wine, and the spring. These dramatic festivals were also competitions, with a prize awarded to the best playwright. The actors, who were all men, wore masks, so they had to rely on their voices and gestures to express feelings. Theaters were often huge, and the actors' gestures must have been exaggerated to be seen from a distance.

THE CHORUS

The chorus was a group of men who sang songs, danced, and spoke as one group. They questioned the actors, commented on the action, and helped explain the play to the audience. These masked actors are the chorus in a modern production of an ancient Greek tragedy.

Chorus members wore identical masks

Carving of a grotesque mask used in a comedy

A muse, or goddess of the arts, offers Euripides a mask

ALL A MASQUERADE

There were often only three main actors performing in a Greek play. Yet thanks to the use of masks, each actor played numerous parts, male and female. The masks' exaggerated features also helped the members of the audience sitting far from the stage to recognize the different types of characters.

FAMOUS AT LAST

The playwright Euripides (484–406 BC) wrote tragedies that dealt with the sufferings of heroes and heroines drawn from myths. In his lifetime, Euripides was not very popular and won the prize for best play only four times. Yet after his death, he was recognized as one of the greatest Greek writers. His nineteen surviving plays are still performed today.

The auditorium

EPIDAUROS

This is the huge Greek theater at Epidauros. It could hold up to 14,000 people, in 55 rows of seats rising up the hillside. Yet it was so well designed that even those in the highest row could get a clear view of the performance and hear every word spoken by the actors. The flat, circular area in the foreground was called the orchestra, which meant "dancing floor." Here the chorus danced to music, while the actors performed on a raised stage farther back.

THE BEST SEATS IN THE HOUSE

These beautifully carved marble seats are in the front row of the Theater of Dionysus in Athens— the oldest theater in the world. The seat on the right, with the paws of a lion, belonged to the priest of Dionysus, the god in whose honor the plays were performed. The others were reserved for important foreign visitors, priests, and officials who had helped to organize the dramatic festival.

CHARIOT RACING

The opening event at the Olympic Games was the chariot race. This was an ancient sport going back to the Bronze Age, when Greek warriors still used chariots to ride to battle. The race was extremely dangerous, for the horses ran at great speed and accidents were common.

Two-horse chariot

THE STADIUM

The athletes entered the Olympic stadium, or running track, through this long, dark tunnel. At the far end, when they walked out into the bright sunlight, they were greeted by the cheers of thousands of excited spectators.

RUNNING RACES

The games included several running events. The short sprint of 650 ft (200 meters) was just one length of the stadium. The long-distance race of 3 miles (4,800 meters) took 24 lengths. The runners here are short-distance sprinters.

OLYMPICS

ONE GREAT LEGACY of ancient Greece is athletics. The Greeks held athletic contests as part of their religious festivals. The most important was the festival in honor of Zeus, held every four years at Olympia—the Olympic Games. Tens of thousands of men traveled from all parts of the Greek world to watch the Olympic Games and to take part. The athletes competed to win fame and honor for themselves and for their cities. The Olympic Games were so important that warfare between Greek states was halted while they took place. This was one time when Greek men could celebrate their common culture and the great god Zeus, whom they all worshiped.

Sprinters running with outstretched arms

THE PRIZE FOR VICTORY
The only prize given to Olympic victors was a wreath of olive leaves. Yet victory brought enormous prestige and fame. Winning athletes brought honor to their states. They enjoyed celebrity status, poems proclaimed their deeds, and statues were put up in their honor.

Olive leaf wreath

Greek discus was made of heavy bronze

Roman marble copy of a lost Greek bronze statue

WRESTLING
Wrestling was a knockout event, in which the winners fought each other until only one victor remained. A wrestler won by making his opponent touch the ground with his knees three times. There were few rules, and wrestlers often tried to break each other's fingers.

DISCUS THROWER
Throwing a discus was part of the pentathlon (five contests), which also included jumping, running, wrestling, and throwing a javelin. The discus sport was forgotten for thousands of years until it was revived in 1896, when the first modern Olympic Games were held in Athens.

Runners always competed naked

SEA BATTLE

In 406 BC, WARSHIPS from Athens and Sparta gathered for their greatest naval battle yet, at Arginusae in the Mediterranean. These ships were triremes—with three tiers of oars, the fastest, deadliest ships of the ancient world. Soldiers stood on deck; rowers strained on their oars below. The battle lasted all day, ships ramming each other with massive bronze-plated prows. By the end, 73 Spartan and 25 Athenian ships were smashed or sunk. The sea was full of wreckage and 20,000 dead or dying men. The Athenians won the Battle of Arginusae, but they would later lose the 27-year war.

EXPLORING THE SEA BATTLE

1 **Trierarch:** *the captain, a wealthy Athenian who paid the ship's costs*

2 **Crew:** *10 sailors, a helmsman to steer the ship, and 5 officers— the state paid the crew's wages*

3 **Marines:** *10 hoplites trained to defend the ship and fight the enemy*

4 **Oarsmen:** *170, rowing in time to a piper's music and at a top speed of 10 knots (10 mph/16 km/h)*

5 **Eye:** *painted on the prow for luck, and still seen on Greek fishing boats*

6 **Mast:** *a square linen sail was used on long journeys, but not in battle*

7 **Archers:** *4 mercenaries (hired soldiers) from Scythia, north of the Black Sea*

8 **Spartan marines:** *armed with javelins, ready to attack the Athenian ship*

9 **Ram:** *wooden prow coated in bronze, for smashing into the enemy's ship*

10 **Man overboard:** *thousands were left to die—5 Athenian generals were executed for leaving them behind*

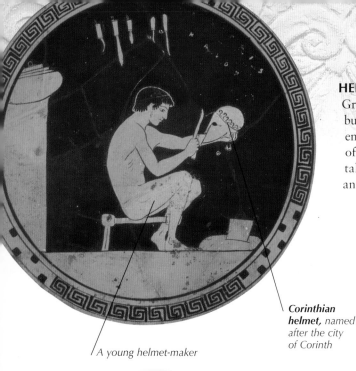

A young helmet-maker

Corinthian helmet, named after the city of Corinth

HELMET-MAKING

Greeks wanted their armor not only to offer protection, but to be beautiful as well. This vase painting shows a youth engraving patterns on a bronze Corinthian helmet—just one of many different helmet styles. It would be completed with a tall crest, made from horsehair and dyed in different colors and patterns, to make a warrior look tall and imposing.

GREEKS AT WAR

THE ANCIENT GREEKS were not a united people. Instead, they lived in numerous separate city-states, which were often bitter rivals. Warfare between the cities was very common. The greatest hatred was between the two most powerful city-states, Athens and Sparta. In the late fifth century BC, the Athenians and Spartans fought each other, on and off, for 27 years. The Spartans, who had the best-trained soldiers, were strongest on land. The Athenians had a powerful war fleet, which they used to control the seas. It was not until the Spartans also built a fleet that they were finally able to beat the Athenians.

Spartan locks

SPARTAN WARRIOR

Unlike other Greeks, Spartan men were full-time warriors. They lived in barracks and spent all their time training for war. Spartan warriors grew their hair long, and carefully arranged it into locks. They said that long hair made a handsome man better-looking and an ugly man more frightening.

Fallen Persian foot soldier

Shield design of Pegasus

Victorious Greek warrior

Spear was used as a jabbing weapon, not thrown

PERSIAN WARS

The Greek city-states would only unite when faced by the threat of a foreign enemy. Early in the fifth century BC, the mighty Persian Empire made three attempts to conquer Greece. Fighting as allies, the Athenians and Spartans defeated the Persian invaders. Once the Persian threat was removed, the Greeks went back to fighting each other.

WAR AT SEA

To defeat Athens, the Spartans had to build a war fleet and learn to fight sea battles. At the battle of Aegospotami in 405 BC, the Spartans made a surprise attack on the Athenians, capturing their whole fleet. Facing starvation, Athens was forced to surrender.

A pair of warships under sail

A GLORIOUS DEATH

Greeks believed that warriors who died in battle gained great glory. Those who met death defending their homeland were honored with public funerals and praised for their bravery. The vase painting above shows a young warrior sitting in a temple-like tomb, surrounded by his weapons and armor.

HOPLITES

The most successful type of Greek foot soldiers were hoplites. They were named after the *hoplon*, the large heavy shield they carried. Hoplites charged toward the enemy in tight ranks, holding their shields closely together for protection. The hoplite's shield was the most important piece of his armor – it defended his neighbor as well as himself.

Horsehair crest on bronze helmet

Hoplites
often chose their own shield design

HOME ENTERTAINMENT

Much of what we know about Greek daily life comes from vase paintings, such as this one showing a banqueting scene. The diners recline on couches, beneath a vine that is heavy with grapes. As they drink their wine, they are entertained by a female musician playing the double pipes. She is a *hetaira* (companion), a woman educated to entertain men.

Eyes were magical protective symbols

Male diner wearing a flowery wreath

***Hetaira** waiting on men*

HAVING A DRINK

Greeks loved wine, which was thought to be the gift of the god Dionysus. The eyes on this drinking cup gaze out from inside a border of ivy leaves— like the grapevine, ivy was sacred to Dionysus. The cup has a pointed base and was probably passed around from hand to hand.

PRIVATE LIVES

THE DAILY LIVES of Greek men and Greek women were very different. Men spent most of their time away from home, meeting friends, exercising at a gymnasium, working, or performing public duties. Women were expected to stay indoors, cook, care for children, give orders to slaves, and spin and weave. Even at home, men and women often lived separate lives. Greek men had dinner parties for their friends—but did not invite their wives. The Athenian statesman Pericles said that, while men competed for fame, "the greatest glory of women is not to be talked about, whether in praise or blame."

Olive tree

OLIVES FOR OIL

Olives were an essential ingredient in a Greek household. They were pressed for their oil, which was used in cooking and burned in lamps to light the home. Olive oil could also be perfumed, and used as cosmetics and medicines. In November, the Greeks harvested their olives by beating the trees with sticks, just as Greeks still do today.

Bronze statuette of a Spartan girl running a race

Bronze mirror hangs on the wall

Woman placing neatly folded linen in a chest

The back of a mirror made of silver and gold

LOOKING GOOD

Although women's social life was limited, some religious festivals gave them the opportunity to appear in public and meet their friends. Before they went out, women took great care over their appearance, carefully arranging their hair and putting on makeup. Those who could afford to wore beautiful jewelry.

Silver chain linking a pair of silver brooches

Two boys and a girl at play

A WEALTHY WOMAN'S QUARTERS

Women had their own separate area of the house, called the *gynaeceum* (women's quarters). This carving gives us a good idea of how it would have looked. From the elaborate decoration on the chest and chair, we can see that this is a wealthy house. Much of the housework, such as cooking, cleaning, and carrying water from the well, would have been done by slaves.

Woman winding thread ready for weaving

BOYS AND GIRLS

While very young, boys and girls lived and played together in the women's quarters. From about six or seven years of age, boys went to a school to learn to read and write, and to a gymnasium to exercise their bodies. Meanwhile, girls were taught at home by their mothers, learning to spin and weave and how to be good wives.

SURVIVAL OF THE FITTEST

Unlike women from other Greek cities, Spartan girls took part in sports. They wrestled, ran races, and threw the javelin. Spartans believed that strong women would give birth to healthy babies. In Sparta, newborn babies were examined by a council of elders. Those judged weak or disabled were abandoned and left to die.

SPINNING AND WEAVING

Most Greeks dressed in clothes that were made at home by the women of the family. Every woman, no matter how wealthy, was expected to spin wool into thread and weave it into cloth. They spun using a weighted stick, called a spindle, and then wove on an upright loom, a timber frame that rested against the wall of every Greek house.

THE ACROPOLIS IN ATHENS

In 480 BC, when the Persians invaded Greece, they destroyed many of its temples—including those on the hilltop Acropolis in Athens. In 450 BC, the Athenian statesman Pericles persuaded his fellow citizens to vote to rebuild the Acropolis. One of Greece's finest architectural showcases, the new Acropolis became a symbol for Athens' power and wealth.

POWER AND POLITICS

POLITICS IS DERIVED from the Greek word *polis* (city-state). While most other ancient societies were ruled by kings, a Greek polis was governed by the citizens themselves. Usually, only the richest or noblest citizens had the right to rule. But the Athenians invented a new type of government called a democracy (people power). Now every Athenian citizen, rich or poor, could make a speech and vote on important issues, such as whether or not to declare war. All public officials were elected or chosen by lot. Even the generals commanding the army were elected by their fellow Athenians. However, women, slaves, and Greeks not born to Athenian parents were excluded from political decision-making.

Marble statue of Socrates (469–399 BC)

DANGEROUS IDEAS

Philosophy means love of wisdom and is another Greek invention. The philosopher Socrates examined the big questions of life, such as "What is truth?" and "How should a man live?" Socrates had many political enemies who thought his ideas were dangerous. They put him on trial for corrupting the young. Found guilty, he was sentenced to die by drinking poison.

This Roman mosaic may show philosophers at Plato's Academy in Athens

Ostrakon naming Aristeides, son of Lysimachus

OSTRACISM

To protect their democracy, the Athenians invented a method known as ostracism to stop any one man from becoming too powerful. Each year, citizens could write the name of a man they saw as a danger to democracy on a small piece of pottery, called an *ostrakon*. The citizen named on the most *ostraka* (with a minimum of 6,000 votes) was expelled from Athens for 10 years.

Ostrakon naming Cimon, son of Miltiades

A solid hub stood for "not guilty"

THE LAW

There were no professional lawyers or judges in ancient Greece. Law cases were decided by juries of ordinary citizens, numbering from several hundred to 6,000, depending on how important the case was. They listened to speeches made by an accuser and an accused, and gave their verdict by voting with bronze disks, indicating guilt or innocence.

PLATO'S ACADEMY

Socrates' pupil, Plato (429–347 BC), set up his own school in Athens, called the Academy. Plato taught here for almost 40 years, discussing philosophy, mathematics, law, and politics with adult pupils. It was probably the world's first university.
Through Plato's writings we know that he distrusted ordinary Athenians and the power that democracy gave them.

A hollow center stood for "guilty"

Upper vessel filled with water

THE WATER CLOCK

A *klepsydra*, or water clock, was used to time the speeches in the law courts. It consisted of two identical pots, one placed above the other. The upper pot was filled with water. Then its stopper was removed, to let the water flow into the lower pot. As soon as all the water had flowed through, the speech had to end. This ensured that each speaker had exactly the same amount of time to make his case in the law courts.

Water flowing into vessel below

KING OF MACEDON

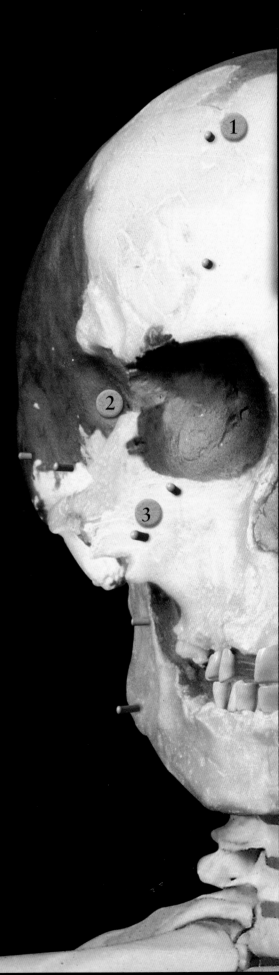

IN 1977, ARCHAEOLOGISTS made an exciting discovery in Macedonia, which lies to the north of Greece. They dug up the rich tomb of a king, whom they identified as Philip II of Macedon. King Philip was a great warrior who forced the Greek cities to unite under his leadership, but he was murdered in 336 BC at the height of his power. Although he had been cremated, the archaeologists found enough pieces of his skull for the dead man's face to be reconstructed. Using wax casts of the bones, scientists made a plaster skull and built up the layers of muscle and skin with clay. After more than 2,300 years, we can once again look at the face of Philip, King of Macedon.

ROYAL ARMOR

When archaeologists entered the royal tomb, they found an outer chamber containing the king's armor. It included a golden quiver for arrows and two greaves (shin guards), one shorter than the other. This was evidence that the tomb was Philip's, because he was lame and walked with a limp.

EXPLORING THE MACEDONIAN KING

(1) Plaster cast: *made from the surviving bone fragments*

(2) Wound above left eye's orbit: *Philip lost an eye when he was hit by an arrow in 354 BC*

(3) Measuring pegs: *indicate the standard thickness of muscle and skin at 23 points around the skull*

(4) Layers of clay: *built up to form the facial muscles*

(5) Golden oak wreath: *found in a casket in the tomb, this may have been worn by the dead man on his funeral pyre*

(6) Waxwork head: *created from the clay reconstruction*

(7) Scar: *Philip's eye wound was said to have been treated by Critobulus, a skilled doctor who caused little scarring*

(8) Hair and beard: *based on two surviving busts of Philip and a coin portrait*

GOLDEN BONE BOX

At the rear of the tomb, archaeologists found this gold larnax (casket). It held the king's bones, wrapped in purple wool cloth embroidered with gold, as well as a golden oak wreath. The starburst on the lid was the emblem of the Macedonian royal family.

FULL OF AMBITION

Alexander's mother, Olympias, claimed to be descended from Achilles, the great hero in the Trojan War. King Philip, Alexander's father, traced his family back to the hero Heracles. Alexander felt that he had to perform great deeds to live up to these famous ancestors, and to his father.

COINING A FACE

Alexander was the first Greek ruler whose profile was shown on coins. Because he conquered such a vast empire, his coins became the most widely used of the ancient world. Even after his death, the kings who followed him continued to issue coins showing Alexander. His distinctive face would have been familiar to everyone, from Egypt to India.

ALEXANDER THE GREAT

ON PHILIP'S MURDER in 336 BC, his 20-year-old son Alexander became king of Macedon, the state that then dominated Greece. After establishing himself as ruler of Greece by crushing all opposition, Alexander gathered a vast army and invaded Asia. A brilliant military leader, Alexander first conquered the Persian empire, which stretched from Egypt to Afghanistan. He then led his army beyond the world known to Greeks, into India. After 11 years of constant campaigning, he had won the largest empire in the world and earned the name "Alexander the Great." In 323 BC, he died of fever in Babylon, his body covered with old battle wounds.

Macedonian pikes hem the Persians in

Alexander in the midst of the battle

INTO BATTLE

This Roman mosaic shows Alexander at the moment of his victory over the Persian king Darius at the Battle of Issus in 333 BC. Alexander, who has just speared a Persian cavalryman, gazes directly at Darius, who looks back at him, frozen in horror, his right hand stretched out helplessly. The terrified Darius will soon flee the battlefield. This dramatic mosaic is thought to be a copy of a lost painting by the great Greek artist Philoxenus.

Alexander *crowned like a medieval king*

Iskander *(Alexander) shielded from the sun by a parasol*

EVERLASTING FAME

Although he only lived to be 32, Alexander achieved his greatest goal in life, which was to win lasting fame. For over 2,000 years, Alexander's story has inspired artists and storytellers. This medieval illustration shows him visiting the oracle of Apollo at Delphi. Alexander is said to have gone there to ask the god for advice before setting off on his campaigns. He was told, "My son, you are invincible!"

Darius *frozen in horror*

Darius' charioteer, whipping the horses, tries to escape

LEGENDS OF THE EAST

Over time, many strange legends gathered around Alexander, particularly in the East, where he was known as Iskander. Here he was remembered as a superhuman figure, who was said to have explored the bottom of the sea in a glass jar and traveled up to the sky in a basket carried by eagles. The illustration above shows Alexander/Iskander traveling as a Muslim king with his army and court.

GREEK MYTHS AND ARABIAN NIGHTS

Greek culture was so influential that it spread outside the Hellenistic kingdoms. Petra, in present-day Jordan, was home to an Arabian people called the Nabateans. Although they were never ruled by Greeks, the Nabateans built Greek-style temples, tombs, and a theater. Here you can see the broken top of their statue of Zeus.

CLEOPATRA

The most famous Hellenistic monarch was Queen Cleopatra VII of Egypt (70–30 BC). This carving, made for her Egyptian subjects, shows her as an Egyptian goddess. In fact she was a Ptolemy, a dynasty of pharaohs descended from one of Alexander's generals.

Sun disk and cow's horns, emblems of the goddesses Hathor and Isis

Vulture, a royal protective symbol

GREEK LEGACY

O N ALEXANDER'S DEATH, his vast empire broke up into several kingdoms, ruled by his generals, who now called themselves kings. This was the start of the Hellenistic Age, when Greek culture spread throughout the ancient world. In far-flung places, from Egypt to the borders of India, people learned to speak Greek, dressed in Greek clothes, and lived in Greek-style cities. They worshiped gods like Zeus and Athena, and went to the gymnasium and theater. In the second century BC, the Romans conquered the Greek kingdoms. Yet the Romans were influenced by Hellenistic ideas, art, and architecture, and passed them to the Western world. As a result, even today we are influenced by the legacy of Greece in countless ways.

THREE GRACES

This Roman wall painting, in the Hellenistic style, shows the Three Graces, goddesses of charm and beauty who were attendants of Aphrodite. Originally sculpted by Greeks, the Graces became a favorite subject for Roman artists. Later, European painters and sculptors such as Raphael, Botticelli, Rubens, Canova, and Burne-Jones also produced their own *Three Graces*.

The boy once held a rein in his left hand

TREASURE AT THE BOTTOM OF THE SEA

Early Greek artists idealized their subjects, giving them perfect features and calm expressions. Hellenistic artists introduced greater realism, so that muscles strain and faces grimace. This bronze horse and rider, dating from around 140 BC, was found in pieces on the bottom of the sea near Cape Artemision, where it had been lost in an ancient shipwreck.

Sculpted muscles and veins stand out on the horse's body

GREEKS, GREEKS EVERYWHERE

If you want to see the legacy of ancient Greece, just look around you. Since the 18th century, public buildings such as museums and libraries have often been modeled on Greek temples. One example is the British Museum in London. It even has statues in its pediment (the triangular space under the roof), just as the Parthenon in Athens once did.

Statues show the progress of civilization

British Museum in London, designed by Robert Smirke and built between 1823 and 1847

Capital, *the horizontal top of the column*

GREEK COLUMN STYLES

Greek architecture followed strict rules, with three main orders, or styles: the Doric, the Ionic, and the Corinthian. Each order had its own distinguishing features. The Ionic Order, used in the British Museum, is easy to recognize thanks to the two scroll-like designs, called volutes, on top of the column.

Index

Acknowledgments

Dorling Kindersley would like to thank:
Andrew Cropper, George M. Georgiou, Andrew Jarvis, and Timothy Mayhew of The Hoplite Association for modeling, Andy Crawford for photography, Hilary Bird for the index.

The publisher would like to thank the following for their kind permission to reproduce their photographs:
Key: a=above; b=below; c=center; l=left; r=right; t=top; ace=acetate; bor=border.

AKG London: 5tr, 11tc, 11bc, 30tl, 31tl, 34tl, 34tr; John Hios 36bl, 21tr, 21bl, 31br; Erich Lessing 12tr, 21tl; Schutze/Rodemann 18tr. **Ancient Art &**
Architecture Collection: 19tl; Ronald Sheridan 23c, 31c. **Bridgeman Art Library, London/New York:** 10c, 11trc, 11bor; Acropolis, Athens, Greece 21br; Ashmolean Museum, Oxford 14cl; 14br, 26tl; British Museum, London 22tr, 29bc; The Detroit Institute of Arts 22b; Louvre, Paris, France 27tr; Museo Archeologico Nazionale, Naples, Italy 18bor, 30c; Musee Conde, Chantilly, France 12br; Museo Nazionale, Taranto, Puglia, Italy 5cr, 29tl; National Archaeological Museum, Athens, Greece 23cl; National Museums of Scotland 26br; Staatliche Museen, Berlin, Germany 18tl; Tarquinia, Lazio, Italy 20tr; Vatican Galleries and Museums, Rome 13br. **British Museum:** 3c, 3bor, 5cl, 6c, bl, 10tl, tr, 11cr, 13tr, 13c, 15tr, 15tc, 16ace, 17bl, 19tr,
19c, 19b, 26bl, 26bor, 27tl, 28tr, 28bl, 28tl, 29tr, 30cl, 38t, 38b. **Cleveland Museum Of Art 2002:** Leonard C. Hanna Jr. Fund, 1991.1. Attributed to the Policoro Painter, South Italy. Lucanian Calyx-Krater, c.400 BC. Red-figure earthenware with added white, red, yellow and brown wash, H. 50.5cm. 7tr (detail), 7br. **Corbis:** Mimmo Jodice 36br; Kim Sayer 37c; Jim Winkley/Ecoscene 16, 16ace. **Gables:** 37bl. Sonia Halliday Photographs: F.H.C. Birch 8, 8-9ace. **Robert Harding Picture Library:** 8, 8ace. © **Michael Holford:** 14tc, 18bl; British Museum 7tl, 15b, 29cr, endpapers. **Kostas Kontos:** 12tl, 32l, 32ace, 33ace. **Metropolitan Government of Nashville:** 2002 Gary Layda 17, 17ace. **The National Archaeological Museum:** 37t. **Stephen Oliver:** 37br. **The Picture Desk:** Art Archive/Antiquarium di Santa Severa
/Dagli Orti 14tr; Art Archive/ Archaeological Museum Naples/Dagli Orti 5bl, 34b; Art Archive/Dagli Orti 6br; Art Archive/Hellenic Institute Venice/Dagli Orti 35tl; Art Archive/ Victoria and Albert Museum London/ Eileen Tweedy Art Archive 35tr. **Photostage:** Donald Cooper 20b. **Royal Ontario Museum:** 4, 17, 17ace. **TAP Service Archaeological Receipts Fund Hellenic Republic Ministry of Culture:** 22tl. **University Of Manchester:** 32r, 32ace, 33ace.
Jacket: AKG London: Erich Lessing spine; Corbis: back tl; Gianni Dagli Orti back tc; Getty Images: Antonio M. Rosario front.
All other images © Dorling Kindersley.
For further information see:
www.dkimages.com
Every effort has been made to trace copyright holders of photographs. The publishers apologize for any omissions.